Just Say No

Because Every Story Needs a Hero

Includes a *Promise Agreement* to Earn
Added Rewards for Saying No to
Binge Drinking, Drug Use, and Smoking
in High School

GARRETT K. SCANLON

Author of *Seeing Past Friday Night*

JustSayNo.org

BALLYLONGFORD BOOKS

Copyright © 2017 by Garrett K. Scanlon

JustSayNo.org
250 Civic Center Dr. 5th Floor CASTO
Columbus, OH 43215

All rights reserved. No part of this book may be reproduced in any manner or form whatsoever, by any means, electronically or mechanically, including photocopying or recording, or by any information or retrieval system, or in relation to goods and/or seminars (including seminars, workshops, training programs, classes, etc.) without the expressed, written permission from the publisher, except by reviewer, who may quote brief passages for reviews or articles about the book.

Disclaimer: The author of this publication is not an attorney and the reader should not consider the information contained herein to be legal advice. The draftsman of the Just Say No Promise Agreement at the end of this book is not an attorney and this agreement is not, and is not intended to be, a legally enforceable contract, but merely an aid for young adults and their sponsors. Reader shall hold Garrett Scanlon harmless from any and all claims, lawsuits, demands, causes of action, liability, loss, damage and/or injury, of any kind. If the reader wants to create an enforceable contract, he or she should consult an attorney.

Names: Scanlon, Garrett K., author.

Title: Just say no because every story needs a hero : includes a "promise agreement" to earn added rewards for saying no to binge drinking, drug use, and smoking in high school / Garrett K. Scanlon.

Description: First edition. | Columbus, OH : Ballylongford Books, [2017]

Identifiers: ISBN: 978-0-9961943-2-7 (softcover) | 978-0-9961943-2-7 (eBook) | LCCN: 2017943395

Subjects: LCSH: Teenagers—United States—Conduct of life. | High school students—Conduct of life. | Peer pressure in adolescence—United States. | Teenagers—Drug use—United States—Prevention. | Teenagers—Alcohol use—United States—Prevention. | Teenagers—Tobacco use—United States—Prevention. | BISAC: YOUNG ADULT NONFICTION / Social Topics / Peer Pressure.

Classification: LCC: HQ796 .S33 2017 | DDC: 305.2/35—dc23

Printed and bound in the United States of America.
First printing 2017. Excerpts are available for reprinting in your publication.

Author is available to speak at your elementary school, middle school, high school, parent group, Rotary, PSR group, church group, and drug and alcohol prevention events.

Visit www.JustSayNo.org

Cover image courtesy of iStockphoto.com
Front cover design: Kristine Coplin
Text design: by www.tothepointsolutions.com

This book is dedicated to that one person ...

Who is not afraid to take on a challenge;

Who has the courage to add some discipline to his or her life;

Who understands that life can be tough, but becomes infinitely easier when we are tough on ourselves;

That one person who dreams heroic dreams;

Who is willing to make a promise, keep it, and upon a job well done, look the other person in the eye, shake hands, and say thank you!

This book is dedicated to that one person—You!

CONTENTS

	A Letter to You	6
1.	Every Story Needs a Hero	9
2.	You Have the Right to Dream Heroic Dreams	13
3.	A Collision Course	17
4.	How I Got the Use of a Car	19
5.	Seeing Past Friday Night	21
6.	And He's My Friend!	23
7.	The Power of Saying No	25
8.	The Great Paradox	27
9.	Incentives and Rewards: The *Just Say No* Promise Agreement	31
10.	Free Samples and Other Sales Tactics	35
11.	How to Prepare for Your Polygraph	39
12.	"What in the World Does Someone Like Me Have to Look Forward To?"	41
13.	Finding Your Guitar	45
14.	The Two Imposters—Triumph and Disaster	49
15.	"I Wish I Had Smoked More Cigarettes."	53
16.	A Letter to Your Future Self	55
	Thank You!	57
	About the Author	58
	How to Bring *Just Say No* to Your Group	59
	Just Say No Agreement with Rewards	61
	Just Say No Agreement—No Rewards	63

A LETTER TO YOU

At ***JustSayNo*.org**, we believe:
- **You are in control,**
- **You are powerful,**
- **You are a hero in the making.**

Up until now, you've had the same friends for many years. You knew all of their parents, the coaches, and the teachers. You were surrounded by a village of great people preparing you for your next journey—high school.

Now it's up to you. The transition from a middle school student to a young, strong, responsible adult has begun. And the stakes are high.

HIGH SCHOOL

Along with an entirely new set of teachers, coaches, and friends, you will be granted a variety of new freedoms. You will learn how to drive a car, possibly get a part-time job, and participate in new activities.

Instead of a village of supporters making your every decision, it will be up to you to make some of the most important decisions of your life. The choices you make now will have enormous consequences for you, well into your future. And like every other young adult your age, all of this comes at a time when you have a relatively low level of experience. Your most *critical* decision will be how well you confront drugs, alcohol, and tobacco during your high school years.

A FALSE SENSE OF SECURITY

In today's world, it is a false sense of security to believe that *society-at-large* will keep you safe from ingesting drugs, alcohol, or tobacco in high school. You cannot rely on strict laws to keep you safe. Because, let's be honest, you can always break the law. You can't delegate the war on drugs to homeland security or law enforcement, because, the bottom line is this:

On Friday night, when you find out that you …

- Were cut from the basketball team,
- Failed that chemistry exam your parents said you better ace,
- Did not get the part in the play you so desperately wanted, or
- Got a text that your girlfriend or boyfriend wants to break up,

And the person next to you says, "Who cares? Let's go get high."

When this happens, the police will not be there. Your teachers will not be there. Your coaches will not be there. Drug counselors will not be there. Even your parents will not be there.

THE GOOD NEWS IS …

No matter *where* you are,

No matter *what time* of day or night it is,

No matter *how often* the critical decisions have to be made,

There is one person who will always be there …

You.

Wherever you go, *you* will always be there! This is a good thing, because *you* are the one person who can *Just Say No*, **every single time**.

It can feel kind of daunting; that it's all up to you. But, isn't it also kind of liberating? It empowers you. Rather than being dependent on a dozen unknown forces out there, *you* can be the hero that keeps you safe. The hero that keeps your brother or sister safe!

Frankly, at *JustSayNo*.org, we believe the war on drugs, binge-drinking, and smoking does not *end* with you. It *begins* with you. It is a confrontation ...

You can win.

You must win.

You will win.

This book is designed to be read in about 30 minutes. It is short, simple, and extremely powerful. It includes a proven plan of action that has worked for thousands of people, along with a *Just Say No* Promise Agreement (in the back of this book) that you will sign with a parent, grandparent, aunt, or uncle that creates added incentives and rewards for you to confront the storm of drugs, alcohol, and tobacco.

No matter your limitations or challenges, you were designed for greatness. You will be somebody's hero. You might not yet be aware of the superpowers you possess, but you will soon discover that they are perfectly suited for a big future.

Read the book, find a guide, and prepare for the storm.

Because every story needs a hero.

Garrett K. Scanlon
www.JustSayNo.org

CHAPTER 1

Every Story Needs a Hero

Any novelist, screenwriter, or playwright will tell you that every story needs **a hero**. The hero is on **a journey**. Then, **a crisis** occurs; an enormous threat or challenge that the hero must defeat or overcome.

Out of a cast of characters, emerges **a guide**; an ally that comes alongside to help the hero. There are always **high stakes** involved. There is a **plan of action** resulting in a **resolute outcome**.

For a story to resonate with us, it must always have these elements. Because, well, that's life!

- **A Hero**
- **A Journey**
- **A Crisis or Threat**
- **A Guide**
- **High Stakes**
- **A Plan of Action**
- **A Resolute Outcome**

In this true-life story, *you* are the hero. You might not *think* you're a hero, because heroes do not always *feel* particularly heroic during their high school years. You haven't even identified all of your super-powers yet! But, you *do* have them. The problem is, those powers don't always apply to what is important to you *right now*.

Some of your greatest skills and abilities that will help you become a great novelist, or entrepreneur, or firefighter, or nurse, or teacher, or Army Ranger, or songwriter are usually unrelated to scoring touchdowns or starring in the school play. You probably don't want anyone telling you, "Don't worry about that. Your day will come." But, what William Shakespeare wrote, is very true: *We know what we are, but not what we may be.*

The Hero: Regardless of any limitations or challenges you have, you are truly designed for greatness. It is your birthright to dream heroic dreams.

The Journey: You are on a *crucial* journey in high school, with a cast of characters that includes new friends, new teachers, and new coaches. You have to juggle a changing physiology, peer pressure, and the emotional swings that occur when you ace a big test one day and get cut from the soccer team the next.

The Crisis/Threat: A storm is coming. A storm that can leave behind a path of incredible destruction. The single biggest threat to you living a powerful life is you making bad decisions regarding the use of drugs, alcohol, and tobacco.

The Guides: Your parents, grandparents, aunts, and uncles are your guides! If you are Rocky Balboa, then they are your trusted fight-trainer, Mickey, who prepared him to survive all 15 rounds. Think about it. They are the ones who are truly in your corner, rooting for you to triumph all 4 years!

The High Stakes: At stake is:
- A loss of respect,
- Team suspensions,

- Loss of friendships,
- DWI's/DUI's/OWI's,
- Attorney fees,
- Suffering grades,
- Loss of car privileges,
- Addiction, and
- A risk that your siblings will follow suit.

The Plan-of-Action: The *Just Say No* Promise Agreement spells out the terms and conditions required for you to defeat the threat and receive added rewards along the way. (You can tear out the Agreements at the back of this book and make copies or download blank Promise Agreements at www.justsayno.org.)

This Story's Resolute Outcome: Rewards begin immediately and victory comes at graduation when you, the hero, shake hands with your guides on a job well done. Like all heroes, you will fulfill the best version of yourself, and your greatest reward will be the strong example you give your siblings, and others, to follow.

The stakes are high. We root for the hero. We root for *you*!

Are you up for the challenge?

CHAPTER 2

YOU HAVE THE RIGHT TO DREAM HEROIC DREAMS

A lot of people think that it was a waste of time to write this book. They echo a lot of what you hear and read from so many self-proclaimed *experts*. Basically, the sentiment is that today's teens are too self-obsessed and screen-obsessed to have a serious discussion about anything important.

You hear things like:

Might as well wait until they're older. They're gonna do what they're gonna do. There's not a whole lot of thinking going on there.

Teenagers are incapable of taking anything seriously. You're talking to them about their future—to a group of people who think they're invincible. Good luck with that.

And, how many times have you heard this one?

Heck, their brains aren't even fully formed until they're 25 years old!

I usually point out that the last time I checked, their brains were fully enough formed to show us how to work the settings on our remote control devices.

Do you buy into those low expectations? I don't. I think the exact opposite is true.

Sure, it might take a bit of time to figure out all of the ground rules, and how you're going to fit into the scheme of things. But, there is nobody out there who wants a bigger life, a more heroic life for yourself, than you do.

In fact, I think that your generation is more fired up about the idea of having a positive impact on others, your family, and the world around you than any other generation in recent memory. And, if there are ideas out there that will help you reach these goals, you're open to listening.

We're told that it's naïve to think that you or your friends have the maturity and fortitude to *just say no* to drugs, alcohol, and tobacco all the time. But, study after study shows that millions of high school freshman, sophomores, juniors, and seniors do exactly that, all day long, every day. Millions! And, we're supposed to believe that you can't be one of those millions? Well, that's just plain stupid. Of course you can! In fact, statistically, the odds say that you *will* be one of those teens who *just say no*.

It is hard to imagine how great life will be for you. You have the good fortune of living in the freest, most prosperous nation, not only in the world, but in the *history* of the world. On top of that, there are tens of millions of baby boomers (born between 1946 and 1964) who will be retiring over the next 15 years, opening up for your generation an endless supply of fulfilling, prosperous career opportunities. And you only need one of them! As much as you enjoy being a teen, you're going to *love* your twenties.

BUT FIRST, THERE IS A STORM COMING.

You didn't create the storm, but it's up to you to weather it. And, if you have a brother or sister, you have to help them get through it too. Because the storm of binge drinking, smoking, and drug use in high school, brings with it the potential for devastating pain. *Physical*, *financial*, and *emotional* pain. It leaves in its path:

- Wrecked cars,
- Serious injury,
- Legal bills,
- Team expulsions,
- Unwanted addictions,
- Poor classroom performance,
- Broken friendships, and
- Harm to your siblings.

And it is headed your way.

THE BEST WAY TO CONFRONT THE THREAT IS TO *JUST SAY NO*.

Not, no *because of this*,

Not, no *because of that*,

No, *because you said so*!

Just Saying No empowers you. *Just Saying No* puts you in control.

The single biggest factor determining your ability to achieve your dreams is not:

- How much money you have,
- How smart you are,
- How attractive you are,
- How good of an athlete you are, or even
- How hard you work.

It is how well you confront the storm ahead of you. There are many rich, smart, nice, attractive, athletic, and hard-working people who have jeopardized their health, career, and family-life by the time they have graduated from high school; all because they didn't recognize that in high school they were on a collision course ...

CHAPTER 3

A COLLISION COURSE

Do you consider yourself to be a good car driver, or someone who *will* be a good driver as soon as you get your license?

You will have taken all of the necessary driving tests, spent time on the road, and are probably a relatively conscientious person. You probably have what it takes to be a good driver. So far, so good?

NOW ASK YOURSELF THIS:

Will you be a better driver four years from now, after you've had 48 more months behind the wheel?

Regardless of age, everyone knows the answer to that question. The more time you spend driving in rain, ice, snow, hail, sleet, high winds, blinding sun, and thick fog, the better driver you become. Driving under different conditions, such as when you are stressed or tired, in mountainous regions, or on long trips; this makes you a better driver.

Because, that is how experience works!

ONE MORE QUESTION:

Do you consider yourself to be good at confronting

drugs, alcohol, and tobacco? You probably are mature for your age and use good judgment. So far, so good?

But, will you have an even better insight after 48 months of watching some of your friends get kicked off sports teams, wreck cars, be cited for DUI's, or injure others? Will you know more after seeing the carnage left behind from a drug overdose? From seeing their younger brothers and sisters follow bad examples?

Sure. Because, that is how experience works.

IT IS NOT A MATTER OF MATURITY!

Your four years of high school might end up being the riskiest and most dangerous four-year period of your life. Likely, you will never again have a time in your life when you are granted such an explosion of new freedoms and responsibilities while having such a relatively low level of experience.

Nobody is saying that you are immature. You are probably more mature than a lot of people who are twice your age.

But, it is not a matter of *maturity*!

It is a matter of *experience*!

DEFY THE VILLAINS.

The best advice you can give yourself is to stay strong for another day. The single act of confronting drugs, alcohol, and tobacco in high school puts you way ahead of the game.

In the meantime, there are real villains in this story who are counting on you making a lot of mistakes.

But, they will be disappointed.

Because, in this story, you are a hero.

CHAPTER 4

HOW I GOT THE USE OF A CAR

It was a sunny day in June, the summer before my freshman year in high school. I had just finished playing basketball with some of the kids in the neighborhood, and was chugging down some lemonade from the fridge when my dad said he had something to discuss with me.

My first thought was, *Uh oh, what'd I do now?* But, from his tone, it didn't sound like I was in any trouble.

"Garry, your mom and I would like to make you an offer."

Hmm, this was weird. I wondered, *what's up with this?*

"As you know, you're going to be starting high school soon, and with that comes a certain amount of added freedom. You are going to be making a lot of decisions when your mom and I are not around. We also recognize that there are going to be a lot of temptations thrown your way. Some of the ones we are most concerned about are drinking and smoking and drugs," he said.

Now I got it. I knew where this was headed. So, I stopped him. "Oh Dad, don't worry about that. I'm not..."

I was about to explain that I knew all about that stuff and that he didn't need to take time explaining it to me, blah, blah, blah. The last thing I wanted was one of those *awkward* talks.

But he interrupted me.

"I am sure you will use your common sense. But this isn't just about you. You see Garry, with all of the things your mom has done for you, and for your brothers and sisters, I can't stand the thought of her having to spend a single minute worrying at night that one of you might get in trouble with any of that stuff. So this is what I'm prepared to do."

The conversation had gone from awkward to serious.

Dad said, "If you agree to not drink, smoke, or try drugs of any kind, then we will make sure that you always have access to a car when you get your license. We will also pay towards the gas and car insurance. And, we'll throw in a reasonable monthly allowance."

I'm sure my dad noticed my eyebrows rise as I tilted my head forward.

I was confused. This had to be some sort of trick. All this, just for skipping out on drugs, alcohol, and tobacco—something I planned on doing anyway? Dad sensed what I was thinking.

"Right now this might seem like an easy thing for you to do," he said. "But four years is a long time and you might find that it becomes more difficult. It's your decision."

"Sure, I'll do it," I said.

We shook hands on it. And I went outside to shoot a few more baskets.

Wow, that was easy, I thought. I had just gotten use of a car.

But my dad knew something I didn't ...

CHAPTER 5

SEEING PAST FRIDAY NIGHT

My dad knew that one of the hardest things for a teenager is *Seeing Past Friday Night* (the title of my first book on this subject). After all, he had once been a teenager.

As you know, high school can be fun, terrifying, exciting, agonizing, boring, exhilarating, confusing, joyful, and even a little bit scary.

Literally overnight, everything is in a heightened state of change. There is a lot of drama with a little bit of chaos tossed in.

PROJECTING PAST HIGH SCHOOL

With all of this happening, it is difficult to project forward and realize that life can get even *better* after high school. It's hard to know that phenomenal things happen in your twenties. Nobody in their twenties ever wishes they could live out high school all over again. But, few teens take the time to consider *anything* beyond the football game on Friday night.

My dad knew this, which is why he challenged me with his proposal. He knew there were suppliers who were intent on targeting me, my brothers, and my sisters for their own profit. He knew the suppliers were counting on the chaos that results from the collision of new freedoms with limited experience.

But, there was something my dad *did not* know when we shook hands and made our agreement ...

CHAPTER 6

AND HE'S MY FRIEND!

Surprisingly, saying no to drugs, alcohol, and tobacco was the easiest thing I ever did. In fact, it sort of became fun. Of course, I didn't let my dad know that (maybe because I thought it would become increasingly difficult to do—which it never really did).

Every time I was offered a beer (always free, by the way), it was a *no-contest* decision. The choice was a beer or use of a car.

Let's see ... can of beer, or car. Let's go with car.

Cigarettes or car. Again, the car wins out.

Pot or car. You get the picture.

But something happened that I never expected. At first, when I declined an offer for a beer or a cigarette, people would want to know why I was saying no.

"Well, here's the deal," I said. "If I don't smoke, or drink, my parents promise me the use of a car and some other incentives."

As you might imagine, most people thought I had a pretty good thing going on. But I will never forget the night a good friend of mine kind of surprised me.

"Hey Scan, how 'bout a beer?"

"Aw, no thanks man. I got that contract-thing going on with my parents."

"C'mon, have one anyway. What's the harm in just having one?" he replied.

"Then the bet's off. I lose the incentives." I said.

"How are they going to find out?" he asked.

I was taken aback that one of the nicest guys I knew, a good friend, was actually suggesting I break my pledge, lie to my folks, and still have them pay for the incentives. And all for a beer? Really?

"You gotta be kidding me," I said. "You'd probably be the first one to tell them!"

Over the next couple of years other friends would occasionally act the same way, and it really made me wonder why it mattered to them at all that I throw in with the crowd and have a beer (I didn't really care if *they* drank or not). I honestly never figured out why some of my friends pressed me on that.

But, I can tell you what ended up being an interesting side effect of *Just Saying No* ...

CHAPTER 7

THE POWER OF SAYING NO

I learned that the world did not end when I said no to a friend who offered me a beer, cigarette, or pot. The universe barely veered off its axis when I set myself apart from the rest of the group.

This taught me an important lesson that I might not otherwise have come to realize; I could stand up to a little bit of peer pressure and be a little different. Over time, something else happened that I didn't expect.

It gave me a quiet confidence.

There is no other way to explain it, but it got me thinking. If I could benefit from standing apart from the group in this small way, what *else* could I do?

By simply denying myself some relatively unimportant things and by resisting some peer pressure, life had become easier and more enjoyable.

There was power in saying no.

And the power was considerable. On top of having a car available to me all of the time:

- I avoided getting a DWI/DUI/OVI and never had to pay those attorney bills!
- I escaped a cigarette habit in high school, saving me big bucks!

- I dodged being a slave to suppliers of drugs, alcohol, or tobacco.
- High school ended up being an incredibly happy time for me, and
- I felt like it enabled me to be a better friend to my classmates.

And my younger brother and sister benefitted too, as they followed my example. The benefits of *Just Saying No* were so powerful, it made me realize that, even if I didn't have a guide, I would do it anyway.

DO IT ANYWAY!

Nobody owes you *anything* for doing these things that you ought to be doing for your own benefit. So, if you can't find a guide, *do it anyway*!

Don't shortchange yourself from a successful future just because you didn't receive added incentives. Living a phenomenal life and being a hero to your siblings is incentive enough.

Always remember that the war on drugs, alcohol, and tobacco does not *end* with you; it *begins* with you.

Because, as you know, there truly is a *Great Paradox* at play here ...

CHAPTER 8

THE GREAT PARADOX

Only by self-imposing rational limitations on our behavior do we achieve true freedom and greatness.

If you want the freedom that comes from being as fit as you can be. That freedom liberates you to:

- Hike Diamond Head in Waikiki to watch the whales,
- Participate in Paralympic events,
- Bike in a peloton event, or
- Ski all day long in Vail, Colorado.

Only by saying no to cigarettes, for example, can you truly do those things *to the best of your ability*.

Performing at your best physically, intellectually, and spiritually is true freedom. It's flat-out liberating! Despite any of your challenges or limitations, being the best version of yourself is nothing less than heroic. It inspires everyone around you.

As every top-performing athlete knows, only by setting

rational boundaries on our behavior can we really have it all! To better illustrate this paradox, let's look at it in *the reverse*.

I KNOW I WASN'T SPEEDING.

A friend of mine was one of the funniest guys I ever met in high school. He had a carefree attitude that was contagious. It wasn't long before people were saying these things about him:

"That guy will say or do *anything*!"

"Did you hear what _____ did Saturday night?"

"He's hilarious. He doesn't care about nothin'!"

Does this describe anyone you know? There is something appealing about a person who goes about things in such a fearless, happy-go-lucky way. Unfortunately, for my friend, he started getting in trouble in little ways, like getting suspended from school for a couple of days.

I didn't really take particular notice until he was quietly kicked off the baseball team junior year. I knew how much he liked playing. A couple of months later, things got a bit more serious. One Friday night, while driving home, he was pulled over by the Highway Patrol.

"Sir, do you know why I just pulled you over?" the officer asked.

My friend answered, "No officer. I know I wasn't speeding."

"No sir, you were definitely not speeding. You were going 32 miles per hour. Unfortunately, the speed limit on this highway is 65. I'm going to have to ask you to step out of the car."

Suddenly, my friend, who was known for 'doing everything', really couldn't do anything. His life of carpe diem—with no limits and no boundaries—had left him with fewer options than any of the rest of us had. He couldn't play baseball, his car privileges were suspended along with his license, and his choices for college were dramatically changed. He spent countless hours working on weekends and in the summer, just to pay for huge legal bills. As you can imagine, he was not at all happy.

This **Great Paradox** doesn't end with high school. Just ask any professional athlete, entrepreneur, doctor, artist, teacher, physical therapist, or business owner of any kind, and they will tell you the same thing:

Sometimes life can be tough, but it becomes infinitely easier when we are a bit tough on ourselves.

Now is the time for you to be intentional. Determine the boundaries you want to set for yourself to achieve the goals that are really important to you. Signing the *Just Say No* Promise Agreement is a great start!

Happiness depends on self-discipline, and self-discipline depends on courage. Have the courage to *Just Say No*.

CHAPTER 9

INCENTIVES AND REWARDS
The *Just Say No* Promise Agreement

Let's face it, if you want a car, there is a good chance that you're going to have to go out and buy one. But, all is not lost! It's time to negotiate. Here are your 5 steps to earning rewards for *Just Saying No*:

Step 1: Show that you are willing to *earn* the rewards. Start from a position of strength and make a pledge that you are personally 100% committed to keeping.

Step 2: Decide who will be your guide(s). Consider parents, grandparents, aunts, and uncles. Spread the pledge and involve more than one guide. It will be easier for them to do, and easier for you to sell what you are proposing.

Step 3: Determine the rewards for success. This is not the time to be greedy or unrealistic. Keep the rewards reasonable and affordable for your guides. Limit the rewards to things that are truly important to you.

My nephew negotiated for a free gas card from his aunt and uncle, partial use of the family car from his parents, and an allowance from his grandparents! Because this agreement was successful, his younger brother got the same deal. When they signed the agreement, I told both of them the same thing, "This will be the easiest *job* you will ever have."

Compare it to the part-time job you could get loading trucks or working at the local grocery store that nets you $7.50 an hour after-tax. The alarm clock goes off at 8:00 a.m. on Saturday morning so that you can get ready to cut grass, answer phones, or flip burgers. Do you really want to go through all that to spend the money on car insurance and your cell phone, if you could instead find a willing guide to help you with those costs in return for simply *saying no*? It's a whole lot easier than cleaning wheels all day down at the car wash. Better yet, keep the agreement *and* the job. You will always have discretionary cash on hand!

Step 4: Clearly identify the penalty for failing to follow through on your promise. Basically, this is an easy one. It is forfeiture of any incentives or rewards. The *Just Say No* Promise Agreement is not intended to be partially kept. What good would that be for any guide?

Step 5: Put it in writing. Read the *Just Say No* Promise Agreement. Make any changes or additions, and be ready to explain it to your guides.

Step 6: Present it to your guides. Let the negotiations begin!

Step 7: Prepare to be your own guide. It is perfectly understandable if you are unable to find a guide who is willing or able to offer you incentives. Most parents and extended family members already have a lot of other financial obligations they need to tend to. But, don't shortchange yourself. Do it anyway! Be your own guide. Invest in yourself! Sign both lines of the agreement. (Or sign a Promise Agreement that does not include rewards.) You will still have an agreement that you have to live up to, and a great excuse to have for your peers.

Step 8: Sign it! Be good to your word. Make your signature mean something! In clear and simple terms, be the hero.

What a powerful day that will be—when you stand at graduation, knowing that you kept this pact with yourself and with your guides. Think about telling *that* story for the rest of your life!

Of course, there will be obstacles ...

CHAPTER 10

FREE SAMPLES AND OTHER SALES TACTICS

Suppliers know the statistics. If they are not able to get you as a customer between the ages of 14 and 18, then they'll probably lose you for good, as a lifelong customer. They also know that if they lose you as a customer, then the odds of them getting your brother or sister as a customer go down dramatically.

That's why they spend millions of dollars each year on free samples. Anyone who has spent years dealing with addiction will tell you that they never had to pay for their cigarettes, or drugs, or alcohol when they first started using. However, they eventually ended up paying thousands of dollars to chase their habits.

During World War II, many of the men and women of the greatest generation were supplied with *free* cigarettes, addicting many of the bravest heroes among us to a lifetime of emphysema, cancer, and heart disease. This was hardly a fitting tribute to these heroes. The cigarette suppliers should have kept their *free* samples.

For some reason, everyone underestimates the marketing savvy of suppliers, as if they just stumbled upon their success in generating hundreds of millions of dollars in profits each year. In reality, they are among the top industries in the world in terms of marketing, production, warehousing, distribution, franchising, and pricing.

Likewise, various illegal drug producers use some of the most talented chemists in the world to create drugs that are more enticing and more addictive. As you know, they even add attractive packaging to make their drugs look appealing to your younger brother or sister!

EARLY ADOPTERS

Suppliers use *early adopters* to introduce their product to a new user group; a new population. Early adopters are often described as people who are the first to engage in high-risk behavior and who are very influential among their peers. They are sometimes viewed as *cool* upper-class students. Oftentimes, they exhibit a bravado that masks an underlying sense of insecurity.

These early adopters frequently have big egos, but relatively low self-esteem. While they exude an attitude of excitement and adventure, they are often acting out against sadness or problems that they are experiencing at home. Because of their hip facade, however, they are able to influence more mainstream teens to use the product and then pass it along to their friends.

THE *NEGATIVE SALE*

Suppliers love to use the *negative sale* strategy, because it is particularly effective. This is where they say, "Oh you shouldn't try it anyway—you're not cool enough to drink." Or, "You're too young to smoke pot," as if sucking smoke into your lungs denotes a certain amount of age-maturity. Or, a popular negative-sale slogan is, "It's probably too dangerous for you." Don't allow yourself to be sucked into using *any* product by the negative sale.

DON'T UNDERESTIMATE THEM!

Don't underestimate their sophistication! They are the ones who approach you ten days after you have surgery for a sports injury to supply you with "replacement pain pills" because your doctor's prescription just expired. They are the ones who influence movie makers to place their products into motion pictures. They are the ones who are sometimes addicted themselves, and need to sell you drugs to fund their own habits.

Take them very seriously. Like *your-whole-life-depends-on-it* serious.

GET LOST!

Remember, if they don't get you, your brother, or your sister as customers by the time you are 18, they have probably lost you for good. So get lost, and make sure your siblings do too!

CHAPTER 11

How to Prepare for Your Polygraph

I didn't know it at the time, but *saying no* also helped prepare me for my polygraph test.

Few people anticipate their polygraph test. If you want to become a police officer, or join one of the branches of the military; or think you might want to work for the C.I.A, F.B.I., Secret Service, or your local fire department, be prepared for this question:

"Have you ever engaged in the sale or purchase of illegal drugs?"

"Have you ever used drugs of any kind?"

"Have you ever committed a crime while under the influence of alcohol or drugs?"

They don't ask you if you have ever *been caught* doing these things!

Police officers can sometimes be forgiven for making a faulty decision, but they are never forgiven *if they lie* about what they did. Here's why. The results of their polygraph are of public record, and even the worst defense attorney will nullify any testimony the officer gives regarding the defendant. The attorney will say, "If they were willing to lie during their job interview to get their current position, how can we trust that they are telling us the truth now?" That is why police recruits who lie are not hired.

So prepare to either answer the questions honestly, or find another career. And if you are going for a job that requires you to travel in a car, or drive a boat, or fly a plane, get ready for:

"Have you ever operated a motorized vehicle while under the influence of drugs or alcohol?" Again, they don't care if you were ever *caught*.

AND DON'T FORGET YOUR FAVORITE FACEBOOK REVIEW!

I was having lunch with a group of social media experts, when a lady at our table mentioned that a new company had recently opened up in her hometown. After a lengthy hiring process, they prepared dozens of written job offers to various candidates.

Only afterwards did the company decide to search the candidate's Facebook pages. They were shocked to find that a third of their candidates exhibited behaviors that were completely contrary to the culture of their organization. Immediately, they sent out letters to 38 individuals, rescinding their employment offer.

Few of the 38 applicants who received the rejection letters (mostly young adults), ever learned the *real* reason for the company's change of heart.

AVOID BECOMING COLLATERAL DAMAGE

It is increasingly more difficult to conceal your behavior just by closely editing what *you* are in control of on social media, because your friends are also taking photos and posting comments about you. *Saying No* might help you avoid having to answer some potentially embarrassing questions.

So begin preparing for your polygraph and your first interview today!

CHAPTER 12

"WHAT IN THE WORLD DOES SOMEONE LIKE ME HAVE TO LOOK FORWARD TO?"

I asked myself this question when I was in high school. I had no idea what I wanted to do once my education came to an end. Who wants to work all the time anyway? I remember feeling intimidated by the idea of someday having to go out and find a job. Having to work *all day long* seemed like such a bummer, so boring, and you didn't even get to take summers off! What a drag that must be.

Maybe you've wondered the same thing from time to time. I remember thinking *what can I do, anyway? It's not like I have any extraordinary skills or anything*. But, that's where I was wrong.

YOU HAVE SUPER-POWERS PERFECTLY SUITED FOR A HEROIC FUTURE

Super-powers rarely apply to the things we like to do in high school. I had a variety of unique abilities, but I didn't notice them a whole lot because they didn't help me set any school track records, or get me a perfect score on the SAT. It wasn't until years later, when it came time to start a career that I discovered I had strengths that were perfectly suited to the field of investment real estate. In high school, I didn't even know what investment real estate *was*!

THE TEACHER

A friend of mine didn't know, until he was 20 years old, that he had an interest in teaching and coaching young adults. Recently, a high school in Cincinnati named their basketball gymnasium after him.

THE CHEF

It was two years after high school that another friend of mine discovered that he had great skills in the kitchen. He ended up travelling the world as a very popular chef.

THE LAW ENFORCEMENT GUY

Having a passion for keeping bullies from harming others isn't a typical trait that propels someone through high school. But it sure came in handy for my brother, a few years later, when he became one of the most highly decorated police officers in the country.

THE REAL ESTATE PERSON

A brilliant friend of mine continues to self-describe himself as having been one of the worst students in his high school class. Yet, he is now one of the most talented developers in Columbus, Ohio, who builds, owns, and operates hotels, office buildings, and athletic clubs.

THE RESTAURANT COUPLE

I remember asking a client of mine how he created one of the most popular restaurants in Columbus. He said, "I went to a banker-friend of mine and told him that I wanted to borrow money to open up a new restaurant. He looked at me and said, 'What in the world do you know about running a restaurant?' I said, 'Nothing. But I *do* know this. My wife, she makes the best lasagna I've ever had!'" Their restaurant soon became one of the most successful in town.

SOME GOOD NEWS!
DEMOGRAPHICS ARE ON YOUR SIDE.

Recently, I asked a large group of young adults what kind of profession they were interested in. As you might guess, there was a wide variety of answers, including: Chef, Veterinarian, Teacher, Firefighter, Physical Therapist, Nurse, Graphic Designer, Filmmaker, Police Officer, Artist, Dog Trainer, Navy Pilot, Musician, Dentist, Writer, Social Worker, Welder, Architect, Oceanographer, Optometrist, and Flight Attendant.

I said, "Good for you. Because your timing is perfect! Your generation of teens is super-positioned to succeed," and pointed out that millions of new careers will open up as the baby boomers retire.

This is one of the reasons why, as great as high school is, you will never say, *I wish I could go back to high school.*

Nope! Not going to happen. High school is a wonderful time. When the time comes to graduate, you will be looking forward to moving on. Because *you're gonna love your twenties*!

Your future is not about all work and no play.

You want to:

- ○ Fly to Chicago on the weekend for a Cubs game with your buddies?
- ○ Spend 10 days vacationing in Europe?
- ○ Mountain-bike through Zion National Park?
- ○ Get involved with play troupes in your area?
- ○ Volunteer to help at-risk children?
- ○ Join the Peace Corps for a couple of years?
- ○ Take up archery, or horseback riding, or fly fishing?
- ○ Try your hand at writing a novel?

It's not all work. The fun and interesting stuff just gets started.

WHY ARE YOUR TWENTIES SO GREAT?

Because, in your twenties you have a lot of experience, combined with new freedoms, fueled by the dollars you earn in your career, topped off with a lot of youthful energy. It's really cool.

There are literally hundreds of examples I could give, of people who were absolutely clueless about what their future would be like, who are doing great and exciting things today. Sure, some of them are exceptional talents, where you could see their success coming from a mile away. But the vast majority of them are just ordinary people, like you and me, who began doing extraordinary things, once they came upon an idea or an opportunity they were passionate about; once they found their guitar ...

CHAPTER 13

Finding Your Guitar

My favorite songwriter is country music artist Brad Paisley, who grew up in the small town of Glen Dale, West Virginia. When Brad was very young, he received a guitar as a gift from his grandfather. It might have seemed like a simple gift at the time, but that guitar became a vehicle that helped propel Brad Paisley to become one of the most popular musical artists of all time.

I sometimes wonder what would have happened if he had never been given that guitar; or if he had instead been given a drum set or a saxophone.

We all need to find our own *guitars*, because …

***Guitars* reveal your super-powers.**

Find a *guitar* that makes the most of your talents, skills, and abilities? For you, your *guitar* might be:

- A set of paint brushes,
- A writer's pen,
- A summer camp for young archeologists,
- A set of golf clubs,
- A biography of a great scientist,
- A fishing rod,

- A camera with black and white film,
- A set of hairstyling tools,
- A summer internship at a law firm,
- A summer job at a local zoo,
- A winter-workshop for aspiring journalists,
- A beekeeper's bonnet,
- A mallet and a chisel,
- An assignment as editor of the school newsletter,
- A book on gourmet cooking,
- A complete set of carpentry tools,
- A book on how to write jokes,
- A scuba outfit,
- A podcast microphone,
- A jigsaw and other woodworking tools,
- A gift of pilot lessons,
- A behind-the-set tour of a movie studio, or
- A chemistry set.

One of my wife's guitars was a sewing machine.

One Christmas morning, I surprised my wife with a brand-new Bernina sewing machine. A year later, she and her best friend opened a small business marketing the beautiful handmade purses and specialty items that they created.

Another one of her guitars was a tennis racquet. With that tennis racquet she joined a tennis team of people who have become some of her best friends. Oh, and she found out that she's really good at tennis!

FINDING YOUR GUITARS

The best way to find *guitars* that will propel you towards your goals and aspirations is to:

- **Take notice of other people's interests and professions.** Observe the interests of your friends, parents, teachers, coaches, extended family, etc. with the idea that some of *their* interests might also resonate with *you*.
- **Involve yourself with a wide variety of school activities.** High school is a great time to participate in the various activities of different groups. There, you might discover which activities match your passion and your talents.
- **Expose yourself to all kinds of different experiences:** Cooking, fencing, volunteering, acting, writing, surfing, painting, etc. The more the better!

Oh, and just because it's a guitar, don't rule out the possibility that your *guitar* might actually be a guitar! It was for Brad Paisley!

CHAPTER 14

THE TWO IMPOSTERS—
TRIUMPH AND DISASTER

The last day of school of my sophomore year, I was helping our history teacher straighten up the classroom. He also happened to be the varsity basketball coach. I had played on the freshman and junior-varsity teams that had compiled a 42-4 record. I was not one of the five starters on the team, but I loved playing basketball, and worked hard at it. Making the varsity team would be great, but I also knew that only six juniors and six seniors made the team each year.

As I was erasing the chalkboard, I said, "Coach, this summer I'm going to play basketball eight hours every day. When I come back next year, you're going to be amazed at how much better I am!"

He replied, "Scanlon, you're cut!"

Ouch.

Knowing how talented the other players were, I was not surprised by his reaction. As hard as I had worked at it, there were simply others who were taller, quicker, or better shooters than me. But it was still a big disappointment. I had been playing basketball all of my life (well, since seventh grade actually—but it *seemed* like forever). Now my career was at an end.

I didn't feel like I had been cut from the team, as much as I felt that the team had been cut out of my life. No more practices, games, or tournaments to look forward to with my buddies. And, it had been such a great way to stay in shape. Now what would I do? How would I fill the time?

I WAS NOT ALONE

Of course, I was not alone. All of my classmates, at one time or another, experienced major disappointments. Maybe they hadn't been selected as editor of the school paper, or voted onto student council. Some didn't get a role in the play that they wanted; others didn't 'letter' in their favorite sport. Disappointments also occurred when there was a breakup of a relationship, or when a fellow classmate relocated to another school.

HOW DO YOU MAKE YOURSELF FEEL OKAY WHEN DISAPPOINTMENTS HAPPEN TO *YOU*?

Honestly, I don't know. Nobody can really 'fix' that one for you. It's such a bummer. However, the Four A's might help you better *respond* to them:

Anticipate: Know in advance that *the disappointments are coming*. They are part of life and they **will** occur (especially in high school). Anticipating this will help you from feeling 'blindsided' by them. *Don't be shocked.*

Assess: See them for what they are. *Keep them in perspective.* They happen to everyone. *Realize that they will not last forever.*

Avoid: *Avoid any tendency to respond in a knee-jerk* way by turning to drugs or alcohol to 'dull the pain'. Think about it, *drugs and alcohol only makes things a whole lot worse*, **never** better.

Appreciate: This is hard to do when you are angry, upset, or frustrated by a setback. But *focus on the things for which you are most thankful*; a best friend, your family, your mountain bike, or violin, for example. Whatever they are, list them on a sheet of paper. *It is impossible to be completely sad and grateful at the same time.*

DEALING WITH DISAPPOINTMENT'S COUSIN— TRIUMPH!

Not only do you have to anticipate extreme disappointment, you also have to be careful of those times of extreme elation.

- You just won the volleyball championship.
- Or the play is over, and you and your classmates were the stars! After months of focused teamwork, it all came together, and you brought down the house!
- Or you just got accepted to West Point, Ohio State, or a top trade school.

Anticipate that there will be times when you are ecstatic. There will be a natural inclination to celebrate. That is when you have to focus, and remember that the celebration is fine; but not if it includes drugs or alcohol. Whatever you are overjoyed by, isn't as important as staying strong to your commitment.

Be careful of the two imposters, Triumph and Disaster. Remember, they are only temporary. Keep them in their proper perspective.

CHAPTER 15

"I WISH I HAD SMOKED MORE CIGARETTES."

My promise to you is this.

Nobody ever looks back on their high school years and says:

- "I wish I had smoked more cigarettes. I'd be a pack-a-day smoker by now!"
- "I wish I had stayed out drinking until 2:00 a.m. more often."
- "I wish I had bought a bunch of drugs while in school."

They don't. And you won't either.

Some people use drugs, alcohol, or tobacco because they think they are going to miss out on something if they don't. They fear they will look back and regret that they didn't partake when they had the chance!

I absolutely promise you that you will never look back and feel as if you missed out on anything. Nobody looks back and wishes they had spent more days fighting off hangovers by sleeping in past noon.

Nobody enjoys the six months they spend working weekends to pay off the attorney they had to hire to defend their DUI (or any of the 'I's), or the $15,000 it costs for a one-month stay in a drug rehab facility.

And *you* will not either!

YOU ACTUALLY MISS OUT ON THE BAD STUFF!

If you confront the storm, you will not look back with serious regrets:

- Did you hurt someone?
- Did you waste a lot of time and money?
- Did you adversely influence the behavior of your brother or sister?
- Did you form an addiction that you have to overcome?
- Did it cost you a college acceptance or a career opportunity?
- Did you do a hundred things that you never intended to do?

Now is the time to write a letter to your future self ...

CHAPTER 16

A Letter to Your Future Self

"Do you ever wish you could travel back in time and have a conversation with your younger self?" That is what a friend of ours asked one day when a few of us were having lunch after playing a couple of sets of tennis. Everyone's answer was unanimous."

"Oh yeah."

Even writing a single letter with advice, back to our younger selves, could be hugely advantageous. Of course, until our quantum physicists figure out a way for us to do that, going back in time will remain impossible. But what about sending your *future* self a letter?

Seriously. Before all of the chaos and drama of high school sets in, why not send your future self a letter saying, "Just get us through these four years safely. We have a big life ahead of us, and most of it happens after high school. *Just Say No* for four short years and then we will take on the world!"

THE CALM BEFORE THE STORM.

Think about it. You're smart enough and mature enough right now to know what you should do. And, you have the advantage of being in the calm before the storm. Your future self might not have that calm.

THE *JUST SAY NO* PROMISE AGREEMENT IS THAT LETTER TO YOURSELF.

We value promises and the people who keep them. Think about the person in your life who you could confide in, knowing that you could trust their promise to keep the conversation confidential. Chances are, the person you just thought of, is one of your best friends or favorite relatives. A promise kept is a very special thing.

So, make a historic promise during the calm before the storm. Write yourself a letter, in the form of a Promise Agreement between you and your guide.

PAGE ONE OF YOUR DIARY?

Let the Promise Agreement serve as the first chapter of your life's story. (Maybe it would be cool to fold it up and put it in the front of the first page of your personal diary.) It is a tangible commitment to your big, heroic future.

Your future self with thank you!

THANK YOU!

Thank you for taking the time to read this book. I hope ...

- ○ You truly understand that, despite any limitations or challenges you have right now, you were designed to live a big life,
- ○ You *always* dream heroic dreams,
- ○ You realize that you have super powers that are perfectly suited for a heroic future.
- ○ You act upon the premise of this book. That you write a letter to yourself in advance that says *keep me safe to fight another day; get me through these next four years safely. I have big things ahead of me*!
- ○ You set a great example for any of your brothers and sisters.
- ○ You remember that when life gets tough, making bad decisions with drugs, alcohol, and tobacco only make things worse. And by setting up rational boundaries you can make your life infinitely better.

But I mostly hope that your high school story has a victorious ending. That you make a promise, keep it, and then, upon a job well done, look your guide in the eye, shake their hand, and say *thank you. That* will be your greatest reward.

What a day that will be. Because, every story needs a hero!

Garrett K. Scanlon
www.JustSayNo.org

ABOUT THE AUTHOR

GARRETT K. SCANLON has served as a volunteer instructor, author, and speaker at middle schools, high schools, rotaries, business organizations, and parent events over the last 15 years.

Since his days as an award-winning Middle School Consultant for Junior Achievement, an experience he greatly recommends to others, Garrett has provided teens with unique concepts and *tangible* tools to help them thrive during their high school years.

Garrett is founder of JustSayNo.org, a website dedicated to helping teens partner with their parents, grandparents, aunts, and uncles to confront binge drinking, drug use, and smoking. The *Just Say No* Promise Agreement continues to inspire students to motivate themselves, months and years after Garrett has left their school.

He is also the author of *Walking and Talking—57 Stories of Success and Humor in the Real Estate World of Business*, Seeing Past Friday Night, *A Road to Bountiful*, and *Single Page Life Plan*.

Garrett is available to speak to school assemblies, parent groups, rotaries, podcast-venues, churches, and drug and alcohol prevention events of any kind.

To learn more, visit JustSayNo.org.

How to Bring JustSayNo.org to Your School, Parent Group, Church, Rotary, SADD/MADD Functions, Web Tribe, Red Ribbon Week, or Prevention Event!

Garrett Scanlon is available to tailor a *Just Say No* Presentation to your group or event. He will bring copies of his books and help your heroes and guides put together a personalized Promise Agreement today!

If you would like to:

- **Schedule** Garrett to speak to your organization,
- **Purchase** bulk-rate copies of *Just Say No*,
- **Subscribe** free to our blog,
- **Get involved** with the *Just Say No* Program,
- **Sponsor** schools to hear the *Just Say No* message,
- **Refer us to groups** who would benefit from *Just Say No*,
- **Donate added rewards** to encourage teens to *Just Say No*,
- **Download a free Promise Agreement**,
- **Provide us with ideas** on how we can improve our message,
- **Tell us your *Just Say No* story**,

Please visit: www.JustSayNo.org

The *Just Say No* Promise Agreement
(JustSayNo.org)

Terms and Conditions:

I, _____ (**Student**) hereby agree to the following promises, beginning today through August 10, 20___ (check all that apply):

- ❏ I will not consume any form of alcohol.
- ❏ I will not use drugs of any kind, in any form, in any way.
- ❏ I will not use tobacco products of any kind.
- ❏ I will not ride as a passenger in a car driven by any person who has consumed alcohol and/or drugs.
- ❏ In the event I find myself in a risky situation and in need of a ride, I will call the sponsor for a ride home.
- ❏ Other (if any): _____
  _____
  _____
  _____

I (We), _____
_____ (**Sponsor(s)**) hereby agree to the following (check any or all that apply):

- ❏ Provide Student with the personal use of a car on the following basis:
  _____
  _____
  _____
  _____

- ❏ Pay for _____% of Student's car insurance, except for any added insurance cost that results from Student being ticketed for a moving violation.
- ❏ Pay for _____% of Student's gasoline expense, not to exceed $_____ per month.
- ❏ Pay for _____% of Student's use of a cell phone, not to exceed $_____ per month.
- ❏ Other (if any): _____
  _____
  _____
  _____
  _____. (*Continued on next page, if checked here:* ❏)

Conditions of Termination: Neither party may take legal recourse of any kind against the other. Sponsor may terminate this agreement if it becomes financially untenable to the Sponsor. Student may not terminate this agreement. The intent of this promise is for it to be fully kept, not partially fulfilled. All parties agree to hold JustSayNo.org harmless, as stated below.*

Penalty for Violation of Terms and Conditions by Student: If Student violates *any* term of this agreement, Student agrees to immediately report the violation to Sponsor(s) who shall, at Sponsor's sole discretion, do any or all of the following:
1. Terminate this agreement making it null and void and of no effect.
2. Temporarily suspend the providing of the incentives stated above, for any time-period that is deemed appropriate by the Sponsor(s).

Further Acknowledgments: Student and Sponsor(s) enter this agreement fully aware of a.) There are many challenges and difficulties that Student will surely experience as a result of peer pressure and other high school pressures, and b.) There is considerable financial cost to Sponsor(s) to provide the incentives contained herein. Both parties enter into this agreement by free will, and without coercion. While there is no inherent obligation of any Sponsor to provide these incentive, Sponsor does so to help Student achieve lofty goals.

Entire Agreement:
No verbal terms or conditions are part of this agreement. This agreement represents the entire agreement. Any changes must be made in writing, and agreed upon by both parties.

Signed this _____ day of _____, 20_____

Student: _____

Sponsor: _____

Sponsor(s): _____

*****Hold Harmless.** Use of this Promise Agreement constitutes consent by all parties that they will fully defend, indemnify, and hold harmless Garrett Scanlon and Just Say No.org from any and all claims, lawsuits, demands, causes of action, liability, loss, damage and/or injury, of any kind whatsoever (including without limitation all claims for monetary loss, property damage, equitable relief, personal injury and/or wrongful death), whether brought by an individual or other entity, or imposed by a court of law or by administrative action of any federal, state, or local governmental body or agency, arising out of, in any way whatsoever, any acts, omissions, negligence, or willful misconduct on the part of Just Say No, Garrett Scanlon, owners, personnel, agents, contractors, or volunteers.

© Copyright 2017, Garrett Scanlon—JustSayNo.org

The *Just Say No* Promise Agreement
(JustSayNo.org)

Terms and Conditions:

I, _____ (**Student**) hereby agree to the following promises, beginning today through August 10, 20___ (check all that apply):

- ❏ I will not consume any form of alcohol.
- ❏ I will not use drugs of any kind, in any form, in any way.
- ❏ I will not use tobacco products of any kind.
- ❏ I will not ride as a passenger in a car driven by any person who has consumed alcohol and/or drugs.
- ❏ In the event I find myself in a risky situation and in need of a ride, I will call the Guide for a ride home.
- ❏ Other (if any): _____

_____
_____
_____
_____

I (We), _____
_____ (**Parents, Grandparents, Aunts, Uncles**) greatly respect student's decision to avoid drugs, alcohol, and tobacco during their high school years, and agree to:

- ❏ Provide transportation to Student in the event Student happens to be in an environment that is unsafe and needs a ride home.
- ❏ Offer encouragement, and requested guidance, as Student walks along this impressive and important path.
- ❏ Other (if any): _____

_____
_____
_____
_____
_____

Conditions of Termination: Neither party may take legal recourse of any kind against the other. The intent of this promise is for it to be fully kept, not partially fulfilled. All parties agree to hold JustSayNo.org harmless, as stated below.*

Penalty for Violation of Terms and Conditions by Student: If Student violates *any* term of this agreement, Student agrees to immediately report the violation to Guide(s).

Further Acknowledgments: Student and Guide(s) enter this agreement fully aware:

- There are many challenges and difficulties Student will surely experience as a result of peer pressure and other high school pressures, and
- Both parties enter into this agreement by free will, and without coercion.

Entire Agreement:
No verbal terms or conditions are part of this agreement. This agreement represents the entire agreement. Any changes must be made in writing, and agreed upon by both parties.

Signed this _____ day of _____, 20_____

Student: _____

Guide: _____

Guide(s): _____

***Hold Harmless.** Use of this Promise Agreement constitutes consent by all parties that they will fully defend, indemnify, and hold harmless Garrett Scanlon and Just Say No.org from any and all claims, lawsuits, demands, causes of action, liability, loss, damage and/or injury, of any kind whatsoever (including without limitation all claims for monetary loss, property damage, equitable relief, personal injury and/or wrongful death), whether brought by an individual or other entity, or imposed by a court of law or by administrative action of any federal, state, or local governmental body or agency, arising out of, in any way whatsoever, any acts, omissions, negligence, or willful misconduct on the part of Just Say No, Garrett Scanlon, owners, personnel, agents, contractors, or volunteers.

© Copyright 2017, Garrett Scanlon—JustSayNo.org

www.ingramcontent.com/pod-product-compliance
Lightning Source LLC
Chambersburg PA
CBHW060355050426
42449CB00011B/2992